Life In A Blink

Words give me strength and power; the kind to keep on moving and fighting another day.

Here's to new beginnings and second chances.

Please treat each poem as an individual piece of poetry. Like mismatched puzzle pieces of time that don't quite fit together.

Read each new poem with fresh eyes and an open mind.

Dedicated to: Papa', Mum, Annamaria, Isabella, Anastasia & Maddison

R I P Papa,

It will never feel real that you're gone, but I know you're in a better place now. I love you more than anything. Thank you for being my biggest fan and pushing me to write more :)

'*As the trees shift*
Softly in the wind,
My breath escapes my chest
Hoping to catch up with yours

There is this constant chill
Lingering in the air
As if you took all
The warmth in your wake.

I always thought
That we would have
Many more memories
That I forgot to enjoy
The ones we already had.

The last words we
Ever exchanged
Never left like that
Always felt like
More to come.

I am sorry
I did not appreciate
All you were offering
When you were around

And that I didn't
hug you tighter
Or hold you that
Little bit longer -

I just never thought
You would leave.'

Battles,
Nasty things they are;
They tempt you,
Craving for your fight
And the passion
Within your bones

And bit by bit,
You lose your light,
The very light that
Has kept you alive
All this time.

Battles In Vain

I am the words that
Accompany the pictures
On the pages

I am the melody
That plays a very
Fine role in a
Movie production

For I am merely a compliment -
Background music,
But never the star.

And I would rather be
Background noise
Than nothing at all.

Background Noise

In a world full of
Broken promises
And empty words,
I found a way to trust you.
In a world full of
Lies and betrayal,
I chose to believe in you.
A mistake I shall never do again.
And sooner or later;
I became as transparent
As the rest of the world.
Alternatively, this is
What happens when
You let your guard down.

The Effects Of Your Actions

As I grew up, I learned that
You had an awful habit of
Lying unnecessarily.

At night I look up at the sky,
Wondering, if you lied that night.
I was only a kid and you told me
I was the moon in
Your brightly lit night sky.

These days I wonder
If you lied then too,
Because I feel more like the
Dimly lit stars that are merely
Forgotten by morning.

Lies Tend To Spiral

I prefer the clouds
Over angry storms any day,
Clouds over the sun
So, the brightness
Does not hurt your eyes.

The storms create those
Kind of loud noises that
Make it hard to
Drown out the
Bad memories
That I continue to
Spend a lifetime
Trying to erase.

Clouds may be safe
But storms make me
Feel as if I will
Never be safe again.

Storms & Clouds

You were my silver lining
In all of this,
And now that you're gone,
What am I going to do
Life was mediocre before you,
Then you came in
On that white horse
And I somehow begun to see
A silver lining in every
Gloomy cloud
That littered my skies,
And without you,
These clouds will rain down
Heavily upon me
And I will no longer hope for
A brighter sky to greet me
In the morning.

Silver Linings

For you, oh god you,
I would stitch all my wounds up
In silly, fancy patterns
Simply in hope of hearing
Your sweet laughter.

And for you,
I would plant dandelions
In the foot of my belly
And wait for them to grow.

All in hopes you would finally see
That it is because of you,
I am beautiful.

Oh dear, for you,
I would sell every possession I own
To buy you a ticket to
A faraway place
So, we can take this
Unforgettable trip.

Elishia C. Xalfa

But the only trouble with all of this
Is that you would cruelly laugh at my
silly wounds
And shake your head with disdain
At the beautiful dandelions.

For you always preferred roses
As common as they may be
And you would rather someone else
On your fancy destinations,
Leaving me alone once more
With all the thoughts
Of what a truly unforgettable trip
This really has been for the both of us.

For nothing in the world
Has ever been enough
Just the way it is
For you.

Never Enough For You

Do you know what the craziest thing
I have ever done in my life is ?
The day I promised,
Not only myself but all those around us
That there was nothing to fix
In our relationship.
When in fact the truth was
Glaring us in the face like some mad
Parent,
As evident as the day,
Just how utterly broken
It all really was between me and you.

Craziest Thing

You never asked for my heart
Which was simply my mistake

But what you chose to do with it
Will always be yours -

You broke it,
Even though you didn't have to.

Our Mistakes

Some days I force myself to remember;
That you are extremely bad for me
And that I deserve far more
Than what you have ever given me.
You lied to me constantly,
Having the nerve to call me crazy –
Making me feel as if I was going insane
Because of all the times I called you out.
This is only one reason,
Number sixty-one,
On a huge list of reasons
As to why I shall never cave
To a man like You again.

Number Sixty-One

LIFE IN A BLINK

I may be ridiculously young to some
Yet startlingly old to others
But in all the years
I have spent on this earth
I have yet to meet another like you.
I wonder if that is a good thing.
I am unsure whether
You're the best thing
Or the worst thing
To ever happen to someone like me.
You are evidently my best mistake
And I will love you
With every irregular beat of my heart
And every unsteady step my feet take.
Until death do us part,

Right?

Best Mistake

Elishia C. Xalfa

I may not have
Been in love with you
But I sure as hell
Loved you more than
The girl who claimed to
And then left you a
Mess and a bottle of pills
To wonder what to do with.

Love Pills

I am sick of every promise
You never intended to keep.
Of all the things you
Put me through,
In hopes I would one day fall.
More importantly, though,
And maybe a little unfortunately,
I have gotten sick of you.
For the time I need to cure
this infection, You.
My departing message
I leave you -
Screw you and your idea
Of who I should be.
I always fell short
And I think that's
Because you don't
Really know me at all.

A Sickness

When I was young
I could not decide
What I would rather grow to be -

A dancer or
A Basketball player.

As a child,
You feel as if
You can do anything
That there is no limit
Other than the one
That of your imagination.

Yet when you grow up,
You begin to lose
That sense of fearlessness
And bravery that once
Resinated inside of your bones

And that in itself
Is a real shame.

A Shame

That day you got in the car,
Mouthing a quick "I love you",
I did not expect you to never come back.
I regret to inform you that I am still
The huge disappointment you always
Thought I was.
Yesterday,
I complained about the amount you
drank,
And yet today,
I have seen the bottom of many empty
bottles.
I can't tell if I'm regular drunk
Or drunk on your love
That felt more like a cage than anything
Else.

Drunk On Love

As I stare outside of
The window of our car,
Watching as the rain
Drops heavily,
I imagine the water like acid,
Burning everything it touches
To nothing more than ash
And strangely,
The thought comforts me.

Drops Of Anger

Do not fall victim
To the complete darkness
Because then it will
Not stop until it consumes
All the light in its wake.

And that is how
Terrible things
Come to pass
And terrible people
Come to be.

In this
We learn who we are
And what we are all capable of.

Light & Darkness

No matter how much time passes,
I still feel the same way about you;
Even if I wish I didn't.
I can't just turn off the way I feel
Because that's impossible.
Pain is meant to be felt and dealt with.
If you were to turn your feelings off,
They would be ten times worse
When you finally decide it's time to feel again.
I still love you, but if you try to come back,
I won't be where you last saw me.
I will be impossible to find
And by then,
The feelings I held for you
Will be unheard of as well.

So, do us both a favour
And leave me alone.

A Problem Fixed With Time

The moment I heard your honeyed voice
Through the phone,
My heart stopped.
Time may claim to heal all wounds
But it lies about the ones made from love.
These ones never fade into scars
For everybody has forgotten how to stop
Playing with old wounds.
Speaking to you again was a mistake
For it only opens a door we struggle to
Close
And neither of us are ready for what it
Has in store for us.
For the sake of our survival,
We must go on alone.
Stop kidding yourself into thinking one
Way or another.
I will be walking down that aisle towards
You.
Times change
And even if wounds don't heal,
I have already begun to change, and the
Pain is almost non-existent now.

Love Wounds

LIFE IN A BLINK

>Once upon a time,
You and I
Were end game
But now the game has changed,
And so will I.
Because people change every day
And sometimes their destinies shift to
Align with that
And if soul mates are a real thing,
You wouldn't be mine.

End Game

People can swear to love you
Till the day they die.
But even the most gullible
Know a lie when they see one -
You cannot make a promise to love
Another until you part this
World forever,
Without knowing what
The future holds,
Without realising the monster
You may become in time.
I watched you become the thing
I was so terrified of growing up -
And that is nobody's fault
But my own
And I'll take that to my grave.

Promises Taken To The Grave

After all the hell we overcome together,
Making memories of a life too painful
To ever look back on,
You walked out that day, bottle in hand,
Swearing you would never return.
It was as if I never mattered,
Even the tiniest bit to you.
I am alone once more
With all of my demons.
I so carelessly obeyed
Every one of your orders,
Like I was running life on autopilot,
Not really living, just sort of existing.
And this felt wrong.
I feel sick to myself
That I ever let myself
Get this heartbroken
Over somebody.
This may be wrong to everyone
But it is what is right for me.
The world believes this is my fault,
So, I shall bear the weight of this
Shipwreck all on my own.

Shipwreck

I can say those three words
A million times and you know what,
No matter how many times
It's spoken of,
Even I can't fully comprehend just how
Much my heart feels for you.
If I don't say it every second,
It doesn't make it any less true,
And even if I say it too much,
The value has not been lost;
I was simply reminding you of all the
Love I hold inside of me,
That is just for you,
And here I am,
Arms wide,
As contradicting
And hypocritical as I can be,
Asking if you can love me too.
But even if you don't,
I'll be okay too.

I Will Be Okay Too

I fought for you every day,
I thought that was what love does.
I thought love meant compromises
And choosing to lose a fight
Rather than having to lose the other.
I thought love meant fighting for someone
No matter how hard it became,
To fight even when it felt futile.
But I was only fighting for your lies,
For the veil of deception,
You had placed over my eyes,
I fought just for you to
Take advantage of me,
And just to be disappointed
All over again.

So, I stopped fighting because
You were not fighting back.
I do not want to fight for someone
Who does not love me in the
Ways that I love them.
I began to fight with myself instead,
To let go of someone who stopped
Holding on a long time ago.

The Fight Of Our Lives

Remind yourself every day;
That someone's poor actions
Are not a reflection of you.
The ill words they speak of others
Shows more about who they are
Than it does the ones they speak of.
What he did to you, sweetheart,
Is not a true reflection of
Who you are as a person
Or what you deserve.
Please stop letting his unfaithful ways
Speak volumes on the kind of person you
Are inside.
His actions never have
And never will define you.

Reminders

You can give someone all of you,
All the best parts,
Even when they have not asked for it
And they will still have the nerve
To throw it right back in your face,
demanding for a better product.
And you, having been gaslit,
Apologise and begin to
Round off your edges
For someone who certainly would not
Appreciate them.
After everything,
Sometimes love is not enough.
It can not magically mend what is broken,
As much as you plead for it to.
For I can't make you love me back
But I can learn to love myself for all my
Imperfections,
And all the things you asked me to change
For 'your love.'

All Of Me

I must love myself even
On the hardest of days,
Especially the days that you think I am
Not worthy to be loved.
I must respect myself enough to walk
Away from a boy
That has not yet learned
How to be a man,
Especially when you can only offer me
Half of what I deserve.
I deserve better,
Better than one's deceitful actions and
Cancerous words that only fill me
With nothing but empty promises.
I deserve honesty and compassion.
I deserve the amount of effort I put in to
Be returned in abundance.
For I deserve love.
The kind of love that is a two-way street,
Not a dead-end alley way.

Love Myself

All I am asking of you
Is that you remember me.
Remember all that we had,
The memories we shared together,
The laughter and the smiles,
Remember the possibility
Of us working out
And that just maybe we could've made it
If you had given it your best shot, the
Way I had given it my all.
And if it's too painful to unlock that
Chest full of hurt,
Then I beg that you
Remember me in even
The tiniest form.

Even if it is in the form
Of an elephant at a zoo
Or when your eyes catch a glimpse of
Your reflection in the morning
Because you knew
That your hair colour was my favourite
Colour of all.
I am okay with being
Nothing more than
A passing thought
For it came for a moment
Which is more than
I could ever ask for
Even if it'll never stay
For more than that.

Remember Me

Elishia C. Xalfa

Sometimes I wish that
We had never met
Because then I would not care.
There is something about you
That binds me to you,
Holding us close forever more.
I do not think I necessarily
Even care about you,
I never spare you
Much of a thought at all.
I forgive you, I do,
But I just cannot forget
What it was that you did
Because that is what
Plays on a lingering loop.
Your actions will
Forever haunt me,
I am second-guessing
Everything I do now
And your words
Echo inside my mind,
Paralysing me, forever so,
Because you take prisoners
To your name, rather than murders

I Am A Prisoner

I would have given the world
To be your cup of coffee
On a good morning
With the rays of sunshine
And the summer breeze
Fluttering through the windows
Illuminating your beauty
In the summer hues
But instead
I became your shot of whiskey
On a bad night
Like tonight
Echoing the storm
Inside of our hearts.

Coffee & Whiskey

No matter how far I run,
How many times I decide
Enough is enough,
How many days may pass without a call,
How many texts go unanswered or how
Many miles lay between us,
Somehow, I still circle
My way back to yours.
I could convince myself of all the reasons
As to why we can't be together
If it were enough to keep me from you.
You are so bad for me and do not deserve
Me even for a second
But somehow at the end of the day, my
Feet will always find
Their way back to you.
I can't run far enough because around
Every corner,
In every song,
In every missing step of the Macarena
And in every star, I look up into,
There you will be
And so, will I.

You Are Everywhere I Look

LIFE IN A BLINK

Nothing was ever enough for you;
The place you worked,
The friends you had,
And me, the girl you were with,
I was not enough for you.
This life was far too simple for you,
The same days over and over,
Nothing changing,
Always standing still on the edge of time.
You were destined to be so much more,
And I was destined to be
Your almost happily ever after -
Your almost decision to have a
Mundane life full of boring routines.
And I, well I, was almost destined to
Settle for a man not quite worthy of my
Love.

Never Enough

In all honesty,
I needed things that even
I had the knowledge that
You could not provide me.
I needed you to do things
You were incapable of.
I desired a person
Who would love me
Regardless of the happenings
Of my darkened past,
And who could love
My mess and a half
As if it were their own.
Unfortunately, it pains me
To admit that I knew all along
It would be impossible for you.
And yet, I kept hoping for you
To have my back anyway,
And you were nowhere to be found.
Every single time.

A Mess & A Half

This is for all the days
You spoke lies about who I was,
Slowly chipping away the best pieces of
Me
Like an ice sculpture that's never quite
Ready -
Never quite enough for You.
For all the days You reminded me
That I shall never be worth anybody's
Love,
That I deserved to be miserable.
I don't care much for Your opinion of
Me,
Because You do not own me;
You never really did.
I am no longer your prisoner,
Held captive by your words
That stung like shackles
Against opened wounds.

Shackles Can Be Broken

If you took a moment
To read between the lines
Written in my very own blood,
You will soon see the truth.

Every word ever wrote
Lines perfectly together
To tell the story of us.

My love for you
Breathes in each chapter,
Finding a way back to you.

The Truth

I may not be some China doll,
Left on some poor unsuspecting
Person's bookshelf
And I may not fall off
When raddled
And yet, I may appear
To be strong on the outside
Made from the strongest
Porcelain products,
But if given just the
Right amount of pressure;
I will be sure to break
Under the weight of it all -
The weight of all that is you.

China Doll

I have been mistreated
Throughout my whole life,
Eespecially by people like you.

I let people take and take
Until I was so empty.
I tried to give you
Everything I believed
You wanted -
Something you could never have.

Somehow, I have spent
More time attempting to
Impress this weary world
And the man who should have
Just been happy I was alive,
Than I ever have of leaving
An impression worth remembering.

I was easily forgotten the moment
You turned your back on us.

The Flower

I'm spending a lifetime
Trying to forget the
Imprints you have left
Scattered along my skin,

Like a badly formed rash
That I just can't itch.

Scars that shine in the
Moonlight, that tell the
Unforgettable story of
What one person can
Do to another without
Thought of consequences.

Imprints

The thing is,
I gave you the power
To make or break me
And somehow,
You still chose to destroy me
Rather than empower me.

I had been searching for a hero
Yet found nothing of the sorts

What lay in the place of my hero
Was nothing more than
A drunken fool.

Unintentional Power

LIFE IN A BLINK

You had an awful habit
Of promising things
You could never, ever keep.

I should have known
They were all empty
And I would have nothing
To show for it all.

You had promised
The world to me
Yet unable to really deliver -

In exchange for obedience
And power over my being.

Empty Promises

Elishia C. Xalfa

There among the carpet,
On the pristine floor,
Lay the shattered pieces
Of my fragile soul -
Laid bare to the world.
My soul may have been crushed,
Broken, and without
A hope for repair
But that didn't mean
That there wasn't
Beauty and love,
Despite all,
Amongst them too.
For my broken pieces
Are what reminds me
That despite the
Way they broke you,
And you broke me in return,
You were still someone
I believed worth saving -

And I still do.

Broken Beauty

I feel like I'm an awful lot
Like you despite your
Absences from my life.

Do you, too, spend your nights
Staring at the bottom of
An empty bottle?

I often choose to believe
That we both feel the same
About those empty cans
Lining the living room floor.

Are you regretting your decision
To leave when we needed you most
Or are you celebrating it ?

I think that it might be the
Difference between us that
I had begged for so many times -

I wasn't a quitter but maybe you were.

Midnight Happenings

I used to see myself as broken,
As a person with missing pieces,
Unable to ever fully be okay again -
And then I met you.

But it's the kind of saving grace you are
That breaks you twice as much
When you too decided to abandon me -
Just like everyone else.

The Devil In Disguise

The scars of my past
Haunt my present
And take my future hostage
Old wounds love to rip open
At the sound of your name
I shout in frustration,
Begging my heart
To let the memory of you be -
To leave it to rest.
Your love has left
The kind of battle wounds
It takes a lifetime to repair.

I Bleed For You On The Daily

LIFE IN A BLINK

A year can make or break two people,
Can either make a love flourish
Or leave havoc in its wake
But for us,
The outcome is clear
Cause now you're just a stranger
Who's laugh I can recognise anywhere.

Stranger Danger

LIFE IN A BLINK

I gave up
On the idea of an 'us'
Lots of yesterday's ago,
Because somewhere between
Now and then,
I realised that it was your fault
We never touched the sky -
Not mine.

The Sky

Elishia C. Xalfa

I loved you
With the kind of love
That sparked the kind of flame
That would never burn out.
The kind of light others envied.
An everlasting bond,
That I was sure would withstand
The sands of time itself.
Not a single soul
Could ever hope to
Replicate it
Nor tear it down.
The way I love people,
Regardless of how poorly
I am treated by them,
Would have to be regrettably,
My strongest asset
Yet also my greatest weakness.
It is the same for the love
I have for you.

Greatest Weakness

LIFE IN A BLINK

I needed you to tell me you loved me -
Because I was desperately
Searching for a man
I knew no longer existed -
But really,
I needed you to tell me
You didn't even more.
Sometimes things hurt in
A way they need to,
In a place that needs to
Ache for a while,
So that it can mould
Us into who we will one day become
And this heartache,
You have caused me,
Is nothing short of that.
For not loving me the way
I begged for,
I say thank you;
I am better off for it.

Bittersweet Truth

Elishia C. Xalfa

LIFE IN A BLINK

You had a nasty habit of
Constantly telling me
I was a work of art,
Simply too beautiful for this world.
You created this idea,
This box, of who you believed I was,
And expected me to live my
Life according to that.
My life wasn't meant to be lived
Inside of a box
Of impossible expectations.
You gave no second thoughts to my
Feelings or ideas,
As if only yours mattered.
Unfortunately,
That is not me.
I am still a work in progress,
I make mistakes,
I change my mind
More times than I can count.
I am stuck in a battle of who I am
And who I would give
The world to be.

And that's perfectly fine,
I still have time
To travel the distance that I seek.
For I never asked to be
Perfect nor your dream girl
But I did want to be
The one doing life by your side.
Someone to settle down with,
To confide in.
I wanted you to never
Look back on your life at sixty
With regrets
Of how your life played out.
But the person you designed me to be in
Your head,
To be your 'perfect bride',
Could never match reality.
I am everchanging and you
Must learn to keep up
If you ever hope to love me.

I Am More Than What the Eye Can See

LIFE IN A BLINK

As the sky turns dark,
And the stars shine brightly,
I try to count them all,
The way we used to
And for every one of them,
I am reminded of you
And how we used to
Admire their beauty together.
And then one
Terrifying thought crosses my mind,
What if I am never on yours ?
That the time that separates us,
Was enough for you to forget
All that we ever said to each other
Was it enough time to forget the promises
We made as well ?
To forget all we did together
I am utterly terrified that I am
Not even a passing
Thought in your mind
As the days race by.

Stars in the Sky

Elishia C. Xalfa

No amount of attention
Or affection
From another
Has ever been quite the same.
I crave things from people
That only you could give me.
I am an addict for your love,
And that is utterly chilling.

A Craving For Your Love

I may have stopped waiting on you,
Knowing you had moved on
But I had never stopped hoping
You'd arrive on my doorstep,
Flowers in hand,
Saying that
Despite our differences
You had never loved anyone more.

Hope Despite All

For you,
My darling,
Are the sun in the
Brightly coloured hues of the sky.
You're the clouds that offer refuge
In an unforgiving summer.
For you,
Are the mesmerising moon on a dark
Night,
The beautiful sky has nothing on you.
You're all the stars combined to me –
But never,
Never are you just one thing
Because one thing
Could never be enough
To explain all that you are.

Your beauty is unmatched
By anything else.

Indescribable Beauty

I will love you
With every aching part of my heart
Till my breath leaves my body
But that does not mean
I will ever give you the power
To ruin me again.

I am no longer
An anchor weighed down
By your rules;
For this ship of
Obedience has sailed.

Obedience Mistaken For Love

When our two worlds collided
It was like a raging storm.
You were the angry cloud
And my tears were the rain of anguish
That spoke so many words that
These lips could never hope to.

Collisions Of The Heart

The more you push me away,
And choose to shut me out,
Even when I have done
Nothing but love you,
It teaches me how to learn
To live without you.
And I may not be there today,
But I will be one day,
Just you wait.

Cut Off From Your Love

At the end of the day,
It was I
Who gave my all
And it was I
Who sacrificed who I was
For a toxic love
Without realising the price
I was paying for it.
Time was delicate,
And I spent it all trying to save you,
From yourself,
Without realising I had lost myself
Amongst the rubble.

The Price For Your Love

LIFE IN A BLINK

As time went on,
And miles lay between us,
My body turned cold.
Echoes of old memories
That cease to make
My cheeks red anymore
For one look from you
Makes me sick to the core
And hardens my heart like ice.
There is no more love inside of me,
To share with the world.
A part of me has grown so cold
That I am unbothered by this fact.
You blew out the fire in my heart,
And left an ice princess in your wake.

Princess Of Ice

You used to tell me
That you were sure
One day I would walk
Out that door
And never return.
You were certain I would
Break you in two,
Never to be whole again.
You were convinced
I would throw you away
As if you were yesterday's trash.
But funnily enough,
That it turned out
To be the other way around.

Ridiculously Ironic

I knew you would leave
Before you ever uttered the words to.
You had stopped looking at me
Like I held constellations in my eyes.
You no longer touched me like
I was a fragile piece of glass
That could break at any time
If not handled with care.
You had long stopped
Talking about me
Like I was your galaxy,
Like there was always more to discover.
I knew you had branched out
And realised the truth;
There was more to the universe
Than just the milky way.

The Milky Way

I did not have a talent
For reading people correctly,
I could never tell how
Someone truly felt,
But I knew in my heart
That people tend to say one thing
And yet always mean another.
I watched you tell me you loved me,
Consistently,
For months on end,
But your actions told
A completely different story.
The truth is;
I knew you were lying to me,
That you only said words that would
Taste nice on my lips,
Hoping your lies would
Be sugar-coated
For easy digestion.
You told me what all girls at seventeen
Begged to hear,
But your eyes burned
With a knowledge unknown to me.

Sugar-Coated Lies

I hope you never return from the war,
Because the war you left at home,
Has already been raged in your absence,
And it found that I am so much stronger
Than you and her ever gave me credit for.
Thank you for taking my best friend
And the man I loved
Away all at once -
Because it paved the way for
Better days,
And smoother nights.
Your absence was
The best present you ever gave me.

A Parting Gift

I realised that
If I didn't forgive you,
For all that you have done to me,
And for the wounds still
Healing into scars,
You would forever haunt me
In my dreams
And in real life
Through faces not quite yours.

Forgiveness

I found that the spark
I always felt with you
Was nowhere to be found.

It was like the passionate fire
We once had inside of our bones
Had burned itself out
When I had stopped checking on it

And I think that's
How we know we've survived
One of the hardest things in our life;
Our first love.
I am free,
Free of you -
Finally.

Surviving You

Here is where the story ends,
I no longer wish to hear from you
The way my bones once begged me to.
I no longer crave the sensation
Of your fingers combing sweetly
Through my curly hair.
The love I held for you once
Has evaporated into thin air,
I no longer grasp for reasons
Why we didn't work -
I gladly let go of the rope
That bound us together.
This time I know that
Loving myself was
The only outcome
For the mess we were -
The best outcome.

Time To Let Go

I have a nasty habit
Of always saying the
Wrong things in situations -
As if I'm incapable of
Replicating a
Compassionate
Sentence.

Face-to-face I am
Cold, closed off from
The world
People think I'm immune
To the interactions
Of humans.

But if you were to
Read the words
Lining my journal
Late at night,
Then you will see
I love so deeply
But feel a brick wall
When trying to
Communicate it all.

Immune

You are more than capable
Of outgrowing the old you,
And changing for the better -

But listen, dear,
There has never been
A single thing wrong with
Who you are now

Do not let the world
Ever tell you otherwise.

Capable Of Change

Do not ever be scared to start over;
Not every ending has to be a bad one.

Let your beginnings be wonderful
And watch the most divine flowers
Grow in the place of your darkest roots.

Divine Flowers

I have come to this startling revelation,
As I laid on the bathroom floor,
Letting the rug soak up my endless tears;

I must learn to love myself more
Than I could ever hope to love you.

Midnight Revelations

For all the times
Each of these petals
Have been burned
To an utter crisp -

I shall vow to regrow
Every one of them
Two times over,

Just to show this world
That I can and will

Rise from these ashes,
Like a Phoenix,
Once more.

Rise